KU-013-407

Contents

▶ Short walks

Introduction

Hiking in the Howgills

Walking in the Yorkshire Dales

People have walked the Yorkshire Dales almost since the first man appeared on our shores. Prehistoric hunters followed regular routes along grassy ridges and across the broad cols connecting individual dales. Later, the Romans built their roads, some of which are now used by modern traffic. Others are still recognisable as stony tracks across the fells. Drovers and packhorsemen, the ancestors of today's long-distance lorry drivers, created green roads which can be traced for miles across the wild central moors. Corpse roads linking outlying hamlets to sanctified ground miles down the dale still exist but it is perhaps the local footpaths, connecting villages and farmsteads, which will give the most pleasure to a walker in the Dales.

Walking is a pastime which can fulfil the needs of everyone. You can adapt it to suit your own preferences and it is one of the healthiest of activities. This guide is for those who just want to walk a few miles. It really doesn't take long to find yourself in some lovely countryside. Most of the walks are five miles or less so should easily be completed in under three hours. Walking can be anything from an individual pastime to a family stroll, or maybe a group of friends enjoying the fresh air and open spaces of our countryside. There is no need for walking to be competitive and, to get the most from a walk, it shouldn't be regarded simply as a means of covering a given distance in the shortest possible time.

What are the Yorkshire Dales?

The Central Pennines are cut by a series of valleys which have become known as the Yorkshire Dales. Radiating from a watershed on the mass of high ground north and east of Ribblehead, five rivers, the Swale, Ure, Nidd, Wharfe and Aire, eventually flow east into the North Sea by way of the Ouse and Humber. Three others, the Ribble, Lune and Eden, all enter the Irish Sea, to the west, as independent rivers. All have their birth on the gritstone cap of the central moors but, with the exception of the Nidd and Lune, they all flow for at least their middle sections through countryside based upon limestone. As a result, the rivers have carved

Short Walks in
The Yorkshire Dales

700037069199

Gu

Published by Collins
An imprint of HarperCollins Publishers
77-85 Fulham Palace Road,
Hammersmith, London W6 8JB

www.harpercollins.co.uk

Mapping generated from Collins Bartholomew
digital databases on the inner front cover and
all walk planning maps

This product uses map data licensed from
Ordnance Survey ® with the permission of the
Controller of Her Majesty's Stationery Office.
© Crown copyright. Licence number 399302

Printed in China

ISBN   978 0 00 735943 1
Imp 001   XJ12504 / UCD

e-mail: roadcheck@harpercollins.co.uk

deep clefts through the soluble limestone rock to reach harder, watertight shales and slates.

Every dale has its own character. In the north, Swaledale is the wildest, a deep-cut gorge below rolling heather moors, joined at Reeth by its even wilder tributary, Arkengarthdale, where the dale begins to take on a gentler aspect. Villages of stone-built cottages line its northern banks. Place names can be traced to the early Viking settlers.

The next east-flowing dale is Wensleydale, the only one which does not take its name from its river, in this case the Ure. Wensleydale was once filled by a glacial lake and its flatter valley bottom and wider aspect is the result. Lush meadowlands feed the dairy cattle which produce milk for the famous Wensleydale cheese. The dale is renowned for its waterfalls but less appreciated features are in its four side dales, all roughly parallel to each other, which flow from the south-west. These often secluded valleys will reward anyone who wants to explore their secrets.

Next is Nidderdale, a little-known dale to the east of Wharfedale, where the strangely-worn shapes of Brimham Rocks cut into the skyline. Nidderdale is not part of the Yorkshire Dales National Park.

Wharfedale and Airdale, with their ease of access from the West Riding, are probably the best known dales. Wharfedale, wooded in its lower reaches, is lined with dramatic limestone formations and attractive villages, a feature echoed by its tributary, Littondale, for all except its sombre headwaters. Airedale's Malham Cove, an amphitheatre of solid limestone, is an outstanding feature of the Dales. A tributary of the Aire flows from its base – the main river still flows underground at this point. The ravine of Gordale Scar, a 'roofless' cave, is close by.

View across Malham National Park

Of the western dales, Ribblesdale is essentially a limestone dale separating the three highest summits of the Dales: Whernside, Ingleborough and Pen-y-ghent. Like the other northern rivers which flow into the Irish Sea, its waters are clean enough to welcome sea trout and salmon. It is the Lune's tributaries, Dentdale and Garsdale which are completely within the boundaries of the National Park, the main dale mostly skirting the north-west edge. Of the Eden, only its highest tributary, Hell Gill with its fantastic ravine, is within the park, its headwaters forming the county boundary of Cumbria and North Yorkshire, a boundary followed by the National Park.

The earliest settlers in the Dales were the hunters who lived in caves such as Victoria Cave above Settle, where the remains of reindeer and bones of grizzly bears have been found, animals which lived on the tundra-like conditions following the Ice Age. With the Roman invasion, roads began to appear across the fells and forts were built to control lead mining areas. Lead increased in value with the expansion of building from Roman times, through the height of monastic power right up to the 19th century when cheaper imports killed off the local industry with devastating effect. Remains of the old lead mines and their smelt houses can still be found on the moors above Swaledale and Wensleydale in the north and near Grassington in the south.

Monasteries developed in the Middle Ages to cement an enforced peace made after the Norman Conquest. With their power, which only ended with the Dissolution in the 16th century, they exploited the riches of the lead mines and encouraged the development of vast flocks of sheep which roamed unhindered for miles across the fells, setting the scene for farming patterns which have changed only in recent years. The next development to take place was the movement of animals and goods across the moors; animals were driven south from Scotland and the Dales by a tough breed of men known as drovers. These men slowly moved their charges to the rapidly growing industrial areas further south, by routes which can still be traced to this day. Many of the old drove roads and pack-horse routes are still clearly defined as 'green roads', which snake for miles across the high fells and limestone plateaux of the Dales.

Geology

Almost 300 million years ago, the rocks which are now the lowest part of the Yorkshire Dales, existed as the muddy floor of a shallow tropical sea. Those muds became slates, the bedrock of many of the Dales' rivers. Gradually the sea filled with the teeming life of tiny crustaceans living amongst long-stemmed waterlily-like plants, called crinoids. As these plants and animals died, their bodies and shells sank slowly to the bottom of the sea, consolidating to form the colossal limestone cover which features so predominantly throughout the Dales. Much later, a huge river delta began to fill this sea, its outer deposits spreading to form shales, and on top of them came the harder gritstones, now the top-most rocks of the highest peaks.

Malham limestone pavement

As all this building up and smothering was taking place, land masses moved and gradually the land which was once in the tropics moved north towards its present position. During all this activity, faults occurred in the surface of the land and the rocks were pushed up and down; Malham Cove is a good example of a fault line appearing at the surface.

While the land was beginning to settle into its present shape, subterranean activity forced hot mineral solutions of ores into narrow cracks in the upper rocks. These mineral solutions were mostly lead but there were traces of silver and even gold. Chemical reactions formed calcium fluoride, which was a nuisance to later miners but is a useful raw material today. To the north, vast upsurges of dolerite created the great Whin Sill.

Around 10,000 years BC, the land, though covered by ice, was beginning to take on the outline of the Dales as we know them. As the ice melted, moraine dams created lakes in areas such as Upper Wensleydale. Mud made from ground down rocks of the high tops began to form the basis of new strata and the process of wearing down and building up began again. In geological time 10,000 years is like a few minutes to us and, once the moraine dams were breached, those muds and clays began to form the basis of today's rich pastures of the Central Dales. The process is continuing.

Wildlife in the Yorkshire Dales

Wildlife habitats follow closely-defined zonal limits; on the high tops of Ingleborough and Pen-y-ghent, habitats are restricted to mosses and a little grass with alpine flowers, such as purple saxifrage (saxifraga oppositifolia), living in tiny crevices and ledges on the limestone crags. Mountains with broader summits, such as Whernside, are able to support coarse grasses, with heather and bilberry dominating the grouse moors further south. Meadow pipits and ring ouzels frequent the higher slopes and the dipper follows streams high on the fell. Birds of prey such as kestrels, merlins and buzzards, as well as the ubiquitous crow, can be found on most of the quieter fells. Mountain hares are often seen

Bilberries

gambolling on the open hillsides. Even though standing water is rare on the normally dry cols and ridges, sea-birds, such as blackheaded gulls, nest far from their 'official' home. For centuries, the land below the 1,700 foot (520m) contour, has been improved for sheep grazing and true native grasses and rushes will only be found in areas of poor husbandry and under-grazing. Mountain pansy (viola lutea), rock rose (helianthemum chamaecistus) and thyme (thymus serpyllum), grow on sparse limestone soils. Limestone pavements are cracked and fissured by 'grikes' where the shade-loving plants such as dog's mercury (mercuriatis perennis) and hart's tongue fern (phyllitis scolopendi) are the remains of ground cover of native ash woods which covered the Dales before the last Ice Age.

Where the riverbanks are uncultivated, natural woodland takes advantage of the rich damp soil and woodland flowers grow in profusion. Many of the rivers have excellent fish stocks but the best by far are the Lune and Ribble and their tributaries. Both main rivers manage to enter the Irish Sea relatively unpolluted and, as a result, are visited by migrant trout and spawning salmon.

The Yorkshire Dales National Park

In many other countries, National Parks are wilderness areas, where few people live unless they are connected with running the park. Countries such as the United States of America have even gone to the length of moving residents off land designated as a National Park. In England and Wales, National Parks are areas of outstanding beauty where people still live and work. One of the major functions of a National Park is to preserve the landscape and the livelihoods of the people living within its boundaries. This is achieved by careful planning control. The National Parks and Access to the Countryside Act of 1949 led to the formation of National Parks in England and Wales.

The word 'National' in the title sometimes leads to misunderstanding. National Parks are not nationalised or in any way owned by the government.

The Yorkshire Dales National Park was designated in 1953 and covers an area of approximately 683 square miles (1769 square km). It is administered by the Yorkshire Dales National Park Authority. The Authority is made up of representatives from the local county and district councils as well as members appointed by the Secretary of State for the Environment.

Large areas of grouse moorland, mainly in the south of the Park, are held by the Chatsworth Estates Trust for the Duke of Devonshire. Rights of Way cross several of the moors but, most importantly, the estate allows free access to Barden and Simonseat Moors above Bolton Abbey on either side of Wharfedale. This means that walkers have the right to roam freely over the moors on all but publicised days during the shooting season or during periods of high fire risk. This concession is one which must be respected by all users.

One of the statutory functions of a Park Authority is the appointment of full-time and voluntary Park Rangers. These are people with particular knowledge of some aspects of the local environment who are available to give help and advice to visitors.

Walking tips & guidance

Safety

As with all other outdoor activities, walking is safe provided a few simple commonsense rules are followed:

- Make sure you are fit enough to complete the walk;

- Always try to let others know where you intend going, especially if you are walking alone;

- Be clothed adequately for the weather and always wear suitable footwear;

- Always allow plenty of time for the walk, especially if it is longer or harder than you have done before;

- Whatever the distance you plan to walk, always allow plenty of daylight hours unless you are absolutely certain of the route;

- If mist or bad weather come on unexpectedly, do not panic but instead try to remember the last certain feature which you have passed (road, farm, wood, etc.). Then work out your route from that point on the map but be sure of your route before continuing;

- Do not dislodge stones on the high edges: there may be climbers or other walkers on the lower crags and slopes;

- Unfortunately, accidents can happen even on the easiest of walks. If this should be the case and you need the help of others, make sure that the injured person is safe in a place where no further injury is likely to occur. For example, the injured person should not be left on a steep hillside or in danger from falling rocks. If you have a mobile phone and there is a signal, call for assistance. If, however, you are unable to contact help by mobile and you cannot leave anyone with the injured person, and even if they are conscious, try to leave a written note explaining their injuries and whatever you have done in the way of first aid treatment. Make sure you know exactly where you left them and then go to find assistance. Make your way to a telephone, dial 999 and ask for the police or mountain rescue. Unless the accident has happened within easy access of a road, it is the responsibility of the police to arrange evacuation. Always give accurate directions on how to find the casualty and, if possible, give an indication of the injuries involved;

- When walking in open country, learn to keep an eye on the immediate foreground while you admire the scenery or plan the route ahead. This may sound difficult but will enhance your walking experience;

- It's best to walk at a steady pace, always on the flat of the feet as this is less tiring. Try not to walk directly up or downhill. A zigzag route is a more comfortable way of negotiating a slope. Running directly downhill is a major cause of erosion on popular hillsides;

- When walking along a country road, walk on the right, facing the traffic. The exception to this rule is, when approaching a blind bend, the walker should cross over to the left and so have a clear view and also be seen in both directions;

- Finally, always park your car where it will not cause inconvenience to other road users or prevent a farmer from gaining access to his fields. Take any valuables with you or lock them out of sight in the car.

Equipment

Equipment, including clothing, footwear and rucksacks, is essentially a personal thing and depends on several factors, such as the type of activity planned, the time of year, and weather likely to be encountered.

All too often, a novice walker will spend money on a fashionable jacket but will skimp when it comes to buying footwear or a comfortable rucksack. Blistered and tired feet quickly remove all enjoyment from even the most exciting walk and a poorly balanced rucksack will soon feel as though you are carrying a ton of bricks. Well designed equipment is not only more comfortable but, being better made, it is longer lasting.

Clothing should be adequate for the day. In summer, remember to protect your head and neck, which are particularly vulnerable in a strong sun and use sun screen. Wear light woollen socks and lightweight boots or strong shoes. A spare pullover and waterproofs carried in the rucksack should, however, always be there in case you need them.

Winter wear is a much more serious affair. Remember that once the body starts to lose heat, it becomes much less efficient. Jeans are particularly unsuitable for winter wear and can sometimes even be downright dangerous.

Waterproof clothing is an area where it pays to buy the best you can afford. Make sure that the jacket is loose-fitting, windproof and has a generous hood. Waterproof overtrousers will not only offer complete protection in the rain but they are also windproof. Do not be misled by flimsy nylon 'showerproof' items. Remember, too, that garments made from rubberised or plastic material are heavy to carry and wear and they trap body condensation. Your rucksack should have wide, padded carrying straps for comfort.

It is important to wear boots that fit well or shoes with a good moulded sole – blisters can ruin any walk! Woollen socks are much more comfortable than any other fibre. Your clothes should be comfortable and not likely to catch on twigs and bushes.

It is important to carry a compass, preferably one of the 'Silva' type as well as this guide. A smaller scale map covering a wider area can add to the enjoyment of a walk. Binoculars are not essential but are very useful for spotting distant stiles and give added interest to viewpoints and wildlife. Although none of the walks in this guide venture too far from civilisation, on a hot day even the shortest of walks can lead to dehydration so a bottle of water is advisable.

Finally, a small first aid kit is an invaluable help in coping with cuts and other small injuries.

Public Rights of Way

In 1949, the National Parks and Access to the Countryside Act tidied up the law covering rights of way. Following public consultation, maps were drawn up by the Countryside Authorities of England and Wales to show all the rights of way. Copies of these maps are available for public inspection and are invaluable when trying to resolve doubts over little-used footpaths. Once on the map, the right of way is irrefutable.

Right of way means that anyone may walk freely on a defined footpath or ride a horse or pedal cycle along a public bridleway. No one may interfere with this right and the walker is within his rights if he removes any obstruction along the route, provided that he has not set out purposely with the intention of removing that obstruction. All obstructions should be reported to the local Highways Authority.

Yorkshire Dales footpath sign

In England and Wales rights of way fall into three main categories:

- Public Footpaths – for walkers only;

- Bridleways – for passage on foot, horseback, or bicycle;

- Byways – for all the above and for motorized vehicles

Free access to footpaths and bridleways does mean that certain guidelines should be followed as a courtesy to those who live and work in the area. For example, you should only sit down to picnic where it does not interfere with other walkers or the landowner. All gates must be kept closed to prevent stock from straying and dogs must be kept under close control – usually this is interpreted as meaning that they should be kept on a leash. Motor vehicles must not be driven along a public footpath or bridleway without the landowner's consent.

A farmer can put a docile mature beef bull with a herd of cows or heifers, in a field crossed by a public footpath. Beef bulls such as Herefords (usually brown/red colour) are unlikely to be upset by passers by but dairy bulls, like the black and white Friesian, can be dangerous by nature. It is, therefore, illegal for a farmer to let a dairy bull roam loose in a field open to public access.

The Countryside and Rights of Way Act 2000 (the 'right to roam') allows access on foot to areas of legally defined 'open country' – mountain, moor, downland, heath and registered common land. You will find these areas shaded orange on the maps in this guide. It does not allow freedom to walk anywhere. It also increases protection for Sites of Special Scientific Interest, improves wildlife enforcement legislation and allows better management of Areas of Outstanding Natural Beauty.

The Country Code
The Country Code has been designed not as a set of hard and fast rules, although they do have the backing of the law, but as a statement of

commonsense. The code is a gentle reminder of how to behave in the countryside. Walkers should walk with the intention of leaving the place exactly as it was before they arrived. There is a saying that a good walker 'leaves only footprints and takes only photographs', which really sums up the code perfectly.

Never walk more than two abreast on a footpath as you will erode more ground by causing an unnatural widening of paths. Also try to avoid the spread of trodden ground around a boggy area. Mud soon cleans off boots but plant life is slow to grow back once it has been worn away.

Have respect for everything in the countryside, be it those beautiful flowers found along the way or a farmer's gate which is difficult to close.

Stone walls were built at a time when labour costs were a fraction of those today and the special skills required to build or repair them have almost disappeared. Never climb over or onto stone walls; always use stiles and gates.

Dogs which chase sheep can cause them to lose their lambs and a farmer is within his rights if he shoots a dog which he believes is worrying his stock.

The moors and woodlands are often tinder dry in summer, so take care not to start a fire. A fire caused by something as simple as a discarded cigarette can burn for weeks, once it gets deep down into the underlying peat.

When walking across fields or enclosed land, make sure that you read the map carefully and avoid trespassing. As a rule, the line of a footpath or right of way, even when it is not clearly defined on the ground, can usually be followed by lining up stiles or gates.

Obviously flowers and plants encountered on a walk should not be taken but left for others passing to enjoy. To use the excuse 'I have only taken a few' is futile. If everyone only took a few the countryside would be devastated. If young wild animals are encountered they should be left well alone. For instance, if a fawn or a deer calf is discovered lying still in the grass it would be wrong to assume that it has been abandoned. Mothers hide their offspring while they go away to graze and browse and return to them at feeding time. If the animals are touched it could mean that they will be abandoned as the human scent might deter the mother from returning to her offspring. Similarly with baby birds, who have not yet mastered flight; they may appear to have been abandoned but often are being watched by their parents who might be waiting for a walker to pass on before coming out to give flight lesson two!

What appear to be harmful snakes should not be killed because firstly the 'snake' could be a slow worm, which looks like a snake but is really a harmless legless lizard, and second, even if it were an adder (they are quite common) it will escape if given the opportunity. Adders are part of the pattern of nature and should not be persecuted. They rarely bite unless they are handled; a foolish act, which is not uncommon; or trodden on, which is rare, as the snakes are usually basking in full view and are very quick to escape.

Map reading

Some people find map reading so easy that they can open a map and immediately relate it to the area of countryside in which they are standing. To others, a map is as unintelligible as ancient Greek! A map is an accurate but flat picture of the three-dimensional features of the countryside. Features such as roads, streams, woodland and buildings are relatively easy to identify, either from their shape or position. Heights, on the other hand, can be difficult to interpret from the single dimension of a map. The Ordnance Survey 1:25,000 mapping used in this guide shows the contours at 5 metre intervals. Summits and spot heights are also shown.

The best way to estimate the angle of a slope, as shown on any map, is to remember that if the contour lines come close together then the slope is steep – the closer together the contours the steeper the slope.

Learn the symbols for features shown on the map and, when starting out on a walk, line up the map with one or more features, which are recognisable both from the map and on the ground. In this way, the map will be correctly positioned relative to the terrain. It should then only be necessary to look from the map towards the footpath or objective of your walk and then make for it! This process is also useful for determining your position at any time during the walk.

Let's take the skill of map reading one stage further: sometimes there are no easily recognisable features nearby: there may be the odd clump of trees and a building or two but none of them can be related exactly to the map. This is a frequent occurrence but there is a simple answer to the problem and this is where the use of a compass comes in. Simply place the map on the ground, or other flat surface, with the compass held gently above the map. Turn the map until the edge is parallel to the line of the compass needle, which should point to the top of the map. Lay the compass on the map and adjust the position of both, making sure that the compass needle still points to the top of the map and is parallel to the edge. By this method, the map is orientated in a north-south alignment. To find your position on the map, look out for prominent features and draw imaginary lines from them down on to the map. Your position is where these lines cross. This method of map reading takes a little practice before you can become proficient but it is worth the effort.

How to use this book

This book contains route maps and descriptions for 20 walks, with areas of interest indicated by symbols (see below). For each walk particular points of interest are denoted by a number both in the text and on the map (where the number appears in a circle). In the text the route instructions are prefixed by a capital letter. We recommend that you read the whole description, including the fact box at the start of each walk, before setting out.

Point of interest —
denoted by a number
in the text

Route instruction —
denoted by a capital
letter in the text

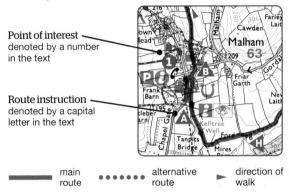

────── main
route

••••••• alternative
route

► direction of
walk

Key to walk symbols
At the start of each walk there is a series of symbols that indicate particular areas of interest associated with the route.

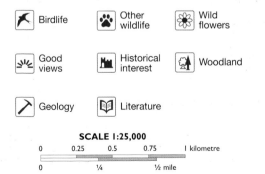

Birdlife

Other wildlife

Wild flowers

Good views

Historical interest

Woodland

Geology

Literature

SCALE 1:25,000

| 0 | 0.25 | 0.5 | 0.75 | I kilometre |

| 0 | ¼ | ½ mile |

Please note the scale for walk maps is 1:25,000 unless otherwise stated
North is always at the top of the page

66 Pleasant stroll which takes in lovely views of Arkengarthdale and Swaledale. The route includes a pretty riverside wood, carpeted with spring bluebells 99

This walk explores part of Arkengarthdale from the village of Langthwaite, a little under 4 miles (6.4km) north of Reeth along the Tan Hill road. Limited parking can usually be found on the main road near the start of the walk. The bridge at Langthwaite, where the walk starts, was used in the opening shots of the popular television series 'All Creatures Great and Small'.

Booze

Bluebell wood

Route instructions

A Take the side turning away from the main road and go over the hump-backed bridge. Cross the square with the Red Lion Inn to one side and fork left on an upward-slanting woodland path.

1 Viewpoint. Langthwaite was the centre of lead mining activity in Arkengarthdale until about 1890, when cheap imports killed off the industry and the valley became de-populated. Scars left by 'hushing', a system where deliberate flooding of part of the hillside revealed the underlying ore-bearing strata, can still be seen on the fells, together with spoil heaps near crushing plant

or mine entrances. The most famous mine is the C.B. on the opposite hillside, named after its 18th century founder Charles Bathurst. **Always take care near the ruined buildings and under no circumstances should the mine workings be entered.**

B Climb to open fields above woodland and go past a ruined farmhouse. Turn right through a wicket gate marked by a finger post. Climb slightly right, uphill along the path marked by posts.

C At the top of the rocky field, go through a gate and follow a track to the right, across the heather moor.

Plan your walk

DISTANCE: 3¼ miles (5.2km)

TIME: 1¾ hours

START/END: NZ005023 Langthwaite

TERRAIN: Easy

MAPS:
OS Explorer OL 30;
OS Landranger 92

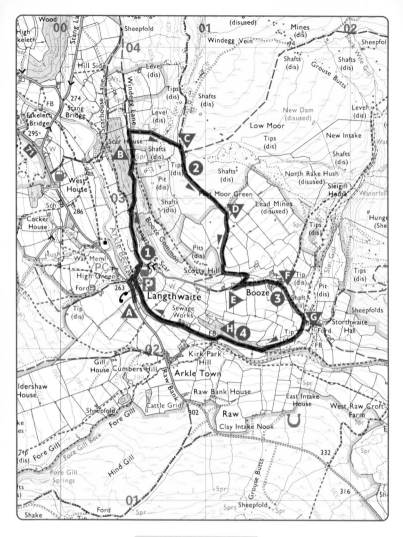

2 Viewpoint. Arkengarthdale is below with Swaledale beyond and to your left.

D On reaching the boundary wall, follow it to the left as far as a barn.

Climb a stile to its right and follow the sunken field path downhill.

E Turn left along the lane into the farm hamlet of Booze.

Booze

3 Booze. The name of this tiny hamlet has nothing to do with alcoholic refreshment – there is not even a pub to be found. It possibly derives from 'bouse', a mining term for undressed lead ore. Narrow and rocky Slei Gill is to the left, a valley which still bears the scars of lead mining.

F Turn right through the stockyard at Town Farm. There is no path but go down the middle of two adjacent fields towards the valley bottom.

G Bear right along a grassy path above the stream then right again into the main valley.

4 The path goes through a pretty riverside wood, which is carpeted with bluebells each spring.

H Do not cross the footbridge on your left but continue upstream along the riverside track into Langthwaite.

Whaw village, Arkengarthdale

> ❝ This easy walk of only 3 miles (4.8km) passes through the villages of Thwaite and Muker ❞

Both of the villages visited on this walk were founded by Norse settlers. Starting in Thwaite near the junction of the Buttertubs Pass road with the B6270 (before the latter climbs into the upper reaches of Swaledale), the route climbs the southern slope of Kisdon Hill with its glorious views of the dale. From Muker (pronounced 'Mooker'), a field path leads back to Thwaite. You can park in the centre of Thwaite although spaces are limited.

Muker & Thwaite

Muker village

Route instructions

A From Thwaite, follow the Pennine Way signs which lead you through the complex of surrounding fields and then uphill above Doctor Wood.

1 Thwaite. The name is Old Norse for a woodland clearing, an indication of the once densely wooded nature of the dale. Some houses still have the remains of outside staircases, a once common feature of Scandinavian farm houses.

B Keep left of Kisdon Farm on a grassy, walled track.

C Turn right at a signpost next to a small barn. Go downhill to join a walled track.

2 Viewpoint of Central Swaledale.

D Go down the farm track, signposted to Muker.

3 Muker village. There are a cluster of stone houses and one pub. Richard and Cherry Kearton, who were wildlife photographers and lecturers in the late 19th and early 20th centuries, were born at Thwaite and went to school in Muker. Working without the advantage of modern film and telephoto lenses, they had to resort to such ingenious disguises as hiding inside a stuffed cow, or artificial tree trunks in order to get their desired shots.

Plan your walk

DISTANCE: 3 miles (4.8 km)

TIME: 1½ hours

START/END: SD891925 Thwaite

TERRAIN: Easy

MAPS:
OS Explorer OL 30;
OS Landranger 98

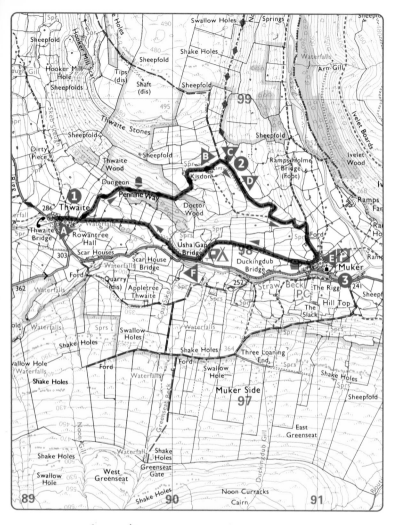

E Do not go as far as the main road but turn right along a narrow back street to reach the open fields. Use stiles to follow the grassy path.

F Join the road beyond Usha Gap Farm and turn right. Do not cross the road bridge but go through a stile on its right and follow a field path back to Thwaite.

Muker & Thwaite

Muker

> 66 Following the valley of the River Bain, this walk takes you to Semer Water which, according to legend, contains a drowned village within its depths 99

The walk is from Bainbridge, a Wensleydale village between Aysgarth and Hawes. Park in the village above a sloping green, seemingly undisturbed by traffic on this busy stretch of the A684. An easy path away from Bainbridge is followed by a mile (1.6km) of road walking which leads to Countersett, where Semer Water is first revealed. From the lake, the return is beside and then above the River Bain all the way back to Bainbridge.

Semer Water

Bainbridge

Route instructions

A Follow the cul-de-sac road away from the village green, past the Dame's School cottage and then along a private drive marked with a footpath sign. Climb away from the house, to the right and into open fields.

1 Bainbridge. After the Norman Conquest, Bainbridge was the headquarters of the Wardens of the Forest of Wensleydale, who were entrusted with guarding it and its game in the name of the king. The only tangible link with that ancient forest, which once covered this part of Wensleydale, is the custom of blowing a horn at 9pm every night from late September to Shrovetide (the week before Lent), in order to guide travellers down from the fells.

2 Viewpoint. The broad sweep of Upper Wensleydale stretches beyond Hawes and towards the blue hazy outlines of the Mallerstang Fells in the west.

B Keep to the right of the large house as indicated by signposts and then cross the dip of the next field.

C Go through the stile to the right of the barn and turn left along the road.

3 Viewpoint. The first glimpse of Semer Water in its moorland setting is revealed as the road begins to descend.

Plan your walk

DISTANCE: 4 miles (6.4 km)

TIME: 2 hours

START/END: SD933903 Bainbridge

TERRAIN: Easy

MAPS:
OS Explorer OL 30;
OS Landranger 98

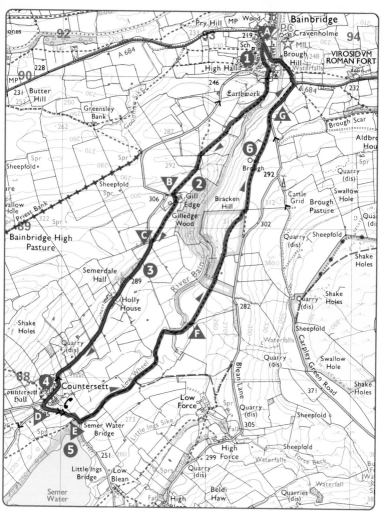

4 Viewpoint. Countersett, a village with long-standing Quaker traditions. 'Sett' is a common ending to place names in this part of Wensleydale. It comes from the Old Norse word 'sætre', which means a permanent or lowland farmstead.

D Bear left through Countersett and follow the road downhill to Semer Water.

5 Semer Water. The lake is a unique occurrence in the limestone dales. It owes its formation to a bed of

Semer Water

impervious slate and a natural dam created by moraine, or debris, left by a retreating glacier. The lake is filled by rivers and streams draining a huge area of moorland to the south-west and, as a result, tiny River Bain, the only outlet for this water, is prone to flash floods, when the lake and river rise with alarming rapidity.

Semer Water has a romantic legend which speaks of a drowned village beneath its waters. The story tells of a traveller who tried to find shelter in the village one wild and stormy night but was refused by all except a poor shepherd and his wife whose house stood beyond the village. The next morning the traveller laid a curse, saying:

> 'Semer Water rise,
> Semer Water sink
> And swallow all the town
> Save yon little house
> Where they gave me
> food and drink'.

Immediately after this curse was laid, a tremendous deluge caused the lake to rise suddenly and drown the village together with all its inhabitants, except for the shepherd and his wife. Strange as it may seem, a Bronze Age village was found when the lake level was lowered as part of a land reclamation scheme in 1937.

Another legend surrounds the large boulder above the pebbly 'beach' near the road. This is the Carlow Stone, reputed to have been thrown there by the devil.

E Go through the narrow stile on the left next to the triple-arched bridge and follow the riverside path signposted to Bainbridge. Keep to the riverbank.

F Climb a ladder stile and bear right uphill. Keep well to the left of the road and follow occasional waymark posts.

6 Viewpoint. Wensleydale is below, its lushness contrasting with the moorland heights of Askrigg Common which fill the skyline. A flat-topped mound on a hillock to the right of Bainbridge is the site of the Roman fort of Virosidum. The Romans came here to exploit the lead ore found beneath nearby fells but would have needed the fort's protection against hostile local Venutian tribespeople. The Roman road from Ingleton to Bainbridge crosses Whether Hill and Cam Fell.

G Join the side road and follow it down to the main road. Turn left into Bainbridge.

> **❝** Spring is the best time for this walk, especially after heavy rain, when the falls are at their most spectacular and the woods and flowers are at their best **❞**

West Burton is a little over a mile (1.6km) to the south of Aysgarth. A series of waterfalls fills the tiny gorge below West Burton and, although just as attractive as their more famous sisters on either side of Aysgarth's mill bridge, these falls are much less well-known. This walk visits both sets of falls and provides the opportunity of comparing their merits. From the National Park car park north of the bridge, the walk is through fields to West Burton, then back via a footpath along the south bank and less frequented section of the Ure. The Aysgarth Falls National Park Centre is on the Carperby Road and is housed in converted railway cottages in a picturesque woodland setting. There is a also a café.

The Waterfalls of Aysgarth & West Burton

View downstream from Lower Falls

Route instructions

A From the car park go down to the road bridge. Climb the steps to the church. Continue by a narrow lane to the main road.

1 Before the walk, you can follow the nature trail to the Middle and Lower Falls. Access to the falls is signposted from the car park. Yore Mill is a Grade II listed building of some historical interest which now houses various retail outlets. High Force is upstream of the mill bridge. Spring is the time for this walk, especially after heavy rain when the woods and flowers are at their best and the falls at their most spectacular.

B Cross the A684 and the stile opposite. Cross six fields, by using stiles in their boundaries, to the road at Eshington Bridge.

C Join the road (Eshington Lane) and cross the bridge. Turn right along a field path, signposted to West Burton.

D Go left and right, along the road through the village.

2 West Burton is built around a wide village green. You can still see the smithy and the Fox & Hounds Inn is to the right of the renovated stocks. A curious spire takes the place of a more conventional preaching cross.

Plan your walk

Barnard Castle
Brough
Kirkby Lonsdale
Skipton
Ilkley
Clitheroe   Keighley
Bradford
Blackburn   Burnley

DISTANCE: 4¾ miles (7.6 km)

TIME: 2½ hours

START/END: SE011887 National Park car park in the village of Aysgarth

TERRAIN: Easy

MAPS: OS Explorer OL 30; OS Landranger 98

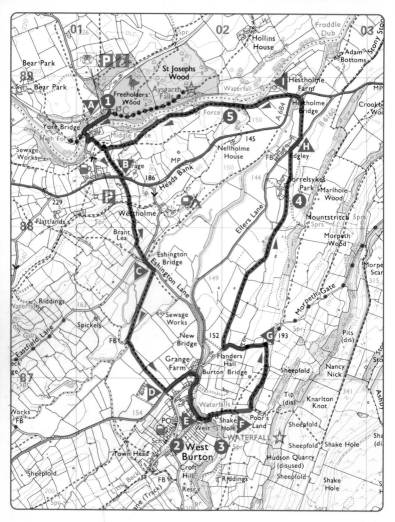

E Follow the lane from the lower part of the green, signposted to 'The Waterfall'. Cross the narrow stone bridge. Then, by path, go left and right uphill.

can be viewed from the footbridge.

F Continue ahead as signposted to Barrack Wood, then left by woodland path.

3 Viewpoint. The waterfall south-east of West Burton

G Turn left down the farm lane and then right by a field

The Waterfalls of Aysgarth & West Burton

path signposted to Edgley. Waymarked stiles and gates mark the route.

4 Twin stone follies on higher ground, off the path to the right, were built by lead miners around 1860. One looks like a pepper pot and was used for smoking bacon.

Turn right along the road for about 130yds (120m), then left through a gate into the last field on the left. Go diagonally across the field to the main road.

Turn left over Hestholme Bridge and right by a waymarked path on its far side. Follow the riverbank to Aysgarth church.

5 Viewpoint. Lower and Middle Falls in their woodland setting.

High Force

> **“** Hardraw Force, England's highest above-ground waterfall is the highlight of this pleasant rural stroll **”**

The starting point for the walk is from the National Park Centre at Hawes car park, in the old station yard. Part of the Pennine Way is then followed across Wensleydale to Hardraw village. After visiting the falls, a quiet field path climbs to Sedbusk village before returning to busy Hawes. A visit to the National Park Centre, also the Upper Dales Folk Museum and possibly the nearby Rope Works, is highly recommended.

Hardraw Force

The village of Hardraw

Route instructions

A Leave the National Park Information Centre and follow the Hardraw road, cutting corners as indicated by the 'Pennine Way' signs.

1 The river is the Ure, a shortened version of Yore, the old name for Wensleydale.

B Climb a steep flight of steps on the left and follow a field path as directed by a 'Pennine Way' sign.

C Turn right opposite the Green Dragon (or left if you have been inside it), then left through the yard of the next house along the road. Climb the hillside by a flagged path.

2 Hardraw Force. The path enters Hardraw village directly opposite the Green Dragon Inn. Go through the bar, first paying a small toll and then out into the wooded gorge leading to the waterfall. The word 'force' is from the Norse 'foss', meaning a waterfall. Bands sometimes play beneath the natural rocky amphitheatre.

3 Viewpoint of Hardraw village and Upper Wensleydale. The Pennine Way leaves the village by the long lane climbing Great Shunner Fell to your right.

D Fork right beside a farmhouse and barn. Walk towards a group of houses.

Plan your walk

DISTANCE: 3½ miles (5.6 km)

TIME: 1¾ hours

START/END: SD875898 Hawes

TERRAIN: Easy

MAPS:
OS Explorer OL 30;
OS Landranger 98

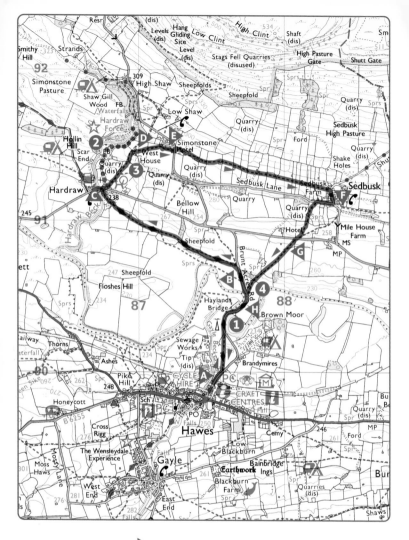

E Cross the road and follow the level drive to the left of the stockyard. Then follow a footpath signposted to Sedbusk.

F Follow the road to the right, through the village and then left at a stile about 100yds (90m) beyond the last house. Go down through three fields.

G Cross the road then over two fields to reach the Hawes road.

Hardraw Force

4 The attractive stone bridge near a clump of trees in the last field prior to the Hawes road is probably on the line of an ancient green road linking villages on the north side of Swaledale. Lady Anne Clifford, Countess of Pembroke, an indefatigable 17th century Dales' traveller, came this way after the Civil War to inspect her war-damaged properties.

H▶ Turn left along the road, again cutting corners by following the Pennine Way path into Hawes.

The River Ure, near Hawes

66 This walk takes in Aisgill summit, the highest
point on the historic Settle to Carlisle railway:
you may be lucky enough to see a steam train **99**

The final upper limits of Wensleydale end in the wild,
little-known moors of Mallerstang Common and the walk is in this
region as far as Hell Gill on the boundary of North Yorkshire and
Cumbria. To reach the start of the walk, drive north-west along
the B6259 (Kirkby Stephen road) for about a mile (1.6km) beyond
the Moorcock Inn. There is some roadside parking and there
are also laybys between the re-planted forest at Lunds and
Shotlock tunnel.

Hell Gill

Mallerstang valley

Route instructions

A Walk down the road, away from the plantation to a footpath sign near the quarry. Turn left across a rough field and follow a waymarked footpath through the wood. Turn right along the forest drive.

1 The abandoned simple stone chapel, to the right of the path, once served this scattered moorland community.

B Follow a signposted footpath to Shaws, the tree-sheltered white house high on the hillside.

2 Shaws stands above a narrow ravine filled by an attractive natural water garden.

C Turn left over the bridge. Then bear right above the house. Follow a faint path up the hillside.

D Climb a stone stile and turn left along the moorland track.

3 The High Way is an old coach road which formerly linked York and Carlisle. The track mostly follows the north side of Wensleydale and can be difficult to trace in places. In its lower reaches below Askrigg, it is now the basis of the modern road.

4 Viewpoint. Wild Boar Fell is on the moors opposite which, at 2323ft (708m), is the highest point of Mallerstang Common.

Plan your walk

DISTANCE: 4¾ miles (7.6 km)

TIME: 2½ hours

START/END: SD789941 Roadside parking and laybys between Shotlock Tunnel and The Quarry on the B6259 (Kirkby Stephen road)

TERRAIN: Moderate

MAPS:
OS Explorer OL 19;
OS Landranger 98

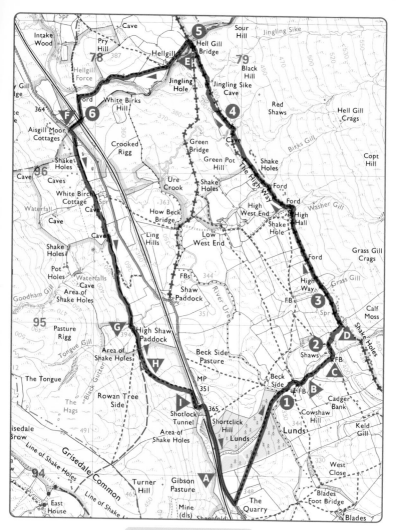

Aisgill Falls on the River Ure can be seen from here and was used as a location in the film 'Robin Hood, Prince of Thieves'.

E ► Cross the bridge and turn left, down the farm track. Cross the railway bridge and continue to the road.

5 Hell Gill Bridge was built to last, once carrying coaches and horses as well a driven cattle. Look over the parapet on either side into the deep chasm

Hell Gill

created by the stream wearing its way through a section of softer limestone.

6 Aisgill summit is the highest point on the historic Settle to Carlisle line, part of the National Rail Network where steam trains run on special occasions.

F Cross the road. Follow a signposted path up to a gate. There is no path, so follow the moorland boundary wall along its right side.

G Go half-right through the abandoned farmyard and, still following the boundary wall, aim for the gate in the corner of the next field.

H Keep level across the pathless moor for about ¼ mile (400m). Then descend gradually to the left, towards the railway tunnel.

I Keep above the portal of Shotlock tunnel. Go through the gate and turn right along the road.

Mallerstang

> **66** Choose a clear day for this walk as, after a fairly strenuous climb, the reward on reaching the summit of Winder is a superb 360° view **99**

As the Matterhorn is to Zermatt, so Winder is to Sedbergh. Boys from Sedbergh School sing of their love for Winder and the friendly protection it offers by sheltering their town from the north winds. The 'i', incidentally, is pronounced short as in 'window'. To the locals, Winder is known simply as 'The Fell' and is an outlier of the glorious rolling hills known as the Howgills. This little-known mass of delectable hills is usually seen, though only fleetingly, by travellers on the M6 or Carlisle to London trains. The walk starts and finishes in Sedbergh, a town built on a southern slope between the Howgill Fells and the River Rawthey. Parking can usually be found in the town centre. As the walk is in open country, it is only suitable for a clear day. Please note that the path beyond the farm at point **C** and the one across the summit of Winder are not rights of way but walkers are normally permitted to use them.

Crook summit

Winder

Glaciated valley
in the Howgills

Route instructions

A Turn right from the car park, then left along the High Street.

B Turn right and follow Howgill Lane to the end of the 30mph limit. Then turn right on a path marked 'To the Fell'. Walk up to Lockbank Farm.

C Go half-right through the farmyard, then left by the grassy path alongside the boundary wall.

1 Viewpoint. Sedbergh is below with Garsdale and Dentdale winding towards the high eastern fells.

D Follow the wall above a pinewood and turn right on a steeply inclined path towards the rounded summit of Winder.

2 Viewpoint. The panoramic all-round view takes in most of the highest Lakeland peaks. To the south and east are Morecambe Bay and the valleys of the Lune, Dent and Garsdale in that order. In the background, you can see the rolling mass of the Howgills.

E Continue ahead and downhill along the grassy ridge to a broad col.

F Turn right downhill, following a well-made path.

3 Viewpoint. The Rawthey valley is below with Sedbergh tucked beneath the foot of Winder.

Plan your walk

DISTANCE: 4¾ miles (7.6 km)

TIME: 2½ hours

START/END: SD657919 Sedbergh

TERRAIN: Strenuous; one climb of 112ft (34m)

MAPS: OS Explorer OL 19; OS Landranger 97 & 98

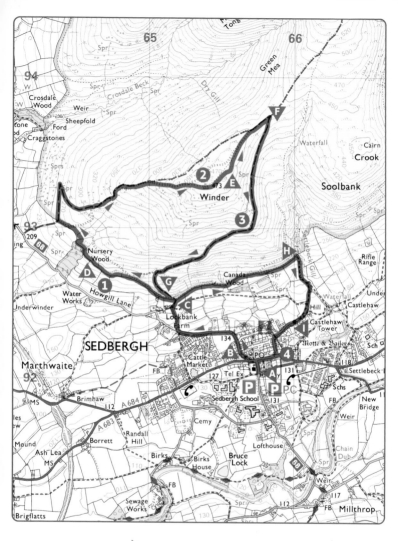

G Go downhill as far as the intake gate at Lockbank Farm. Turn left away from the farm, again following the fell boundary wall.

H Turn right through a kissing gate and walk

downhill to the right of a shaley wooded gorge.

I Follow the farm lane to the right into the outskirts of Sedbergh. The church and central car parks are on the right of the town centre.

Winder

4 It is possible to extend this walk by following walk 8 (Sedbergh & the River Rawthey); the valley and riverside walk will make an interesting contrast to the ascent of Winder.

Hiking in the Howgills

> **"There are good views of the Howgill Fells from the banks of the River Rawthey"**

The pleasant market town of Sedbergh, only a few miles from the Lake District National Park, has an atmosphere more akin to the Lake District than the towns and villages of the dales to the east. Sheltered by the Howgill Fells to its north, Sedbergh has a sunny aspect and has the added attraction of having the Rawthey, a fine trout river and a tributary of the Lune, running just to the south. There are parking facilities in the town centre and access is via the A683 Kirkby Stephen road or the A684 from Wensleydale. This walk can be extended by joining it to walk 7, which begins and ends in Sedbergh.

Landscape near Sedbergh

Sedbergh & the River Rawthey

Sedbergh School

Plan your walk

DISTANCE: 4½ miles (7.2 km)

TIME: 2¼ hours

START/END: SD657919 Sedbergh

TERRAIN: Easy / Moderate

MAPS:
OS Explorer OL 19;
OS Landranger 97 & 98

Route instructions

A From the car park, walk to the right along Main Street for about 80yds (73m), passing the Information Centre.

B Turn left to follow a narrow lane opposite the converging road junction.

1 The double mound on the right is a Motte & Bailey, the remains of a stockade fort probably built in the 11th century.

C Bear right at Castlehaw Farm and past Howgill Bunk Barn, into open fields. Keep to the left of the boundary wall but change sides at a stile next to a massive upright stone within the wall.

2 Viewpoint looking across the Rawthey Valley into Garsdale.

D Turn right at Ghyll Farm and walk down the concrete lane.

E Bear left around Stone Hall, go through a gate, turn left again and follow a boundary wall downhill.

F Follow the field path to the right of Hollin Hill Farm.

G Bear right at the side of the large white house and then walk down its access drive.

H Follow yellow waymarks to the left through the stockyard at Buckbank.

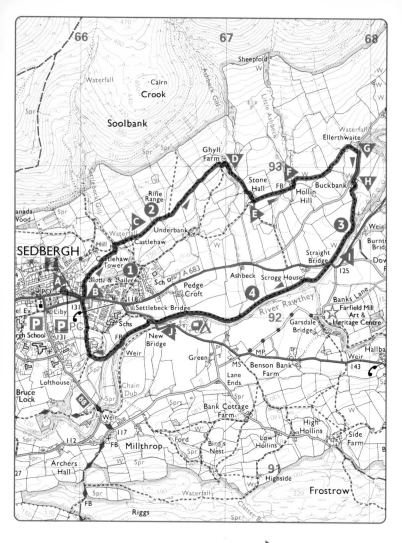

Follow the hedge downhill to the road bridge.

3 Viewpoint. Frostow Fells are opposite above the confluence of Garsdale's Clough River and the Rawthey stream.

▶ Cross the road, climb the stile and follow the riverside path downstream.

4 Viewpoint. Sedbergh is to your left, backed by the mass of the Howgill Fells.

Sedbergh & the River Rawthey

Cross the Garsdale road and continue to follow the riverbank. Turn right with the path and climb past a school building, then beside the rugby field into Sedbergh. The town centre is to the left.

Sedbergh

> 66 The imposing ruins of Middleham Castle, once home of Richard, Duke of Gloucester, before he became King Richard III, are worth viewing 99

Richard, Duke of Gloucester, Yorkist and future King Richard III (1452-1485), once lived in the imposing Norman Castle which still dominates Middleham. Its towering bulk remains a true memorial to the master masons who erected it more than eight centuries ago.

Middleham, the Newmarket of the North, is the centre of a bloodstock breeding area with a dozen or so trainers handling hundreds of potentially top-class racehorses.

About a mile (1.6km) beyond Middleham towards Leybum, the road crosses the River Ure by an imposing iron girder bridge, which was built by public subscription in 1850, replacing a suspension bridge which collapsed in 1831 after only two years' use. Below the town, in Swaledale, the River Ure, which is now joined by the Cover, widens as it reaches the broad acres of the Vale of York. The dale's character becomes more wooded in its flatter, lower reaches. About 3 miles (4.8 km) from Middleham along the Masham Road, you will find the ruins of Jervaulx Abbey. During the life of this abbey, the Cistercian monks who lived there became famous for their cheese, a forerunner of Wensleydale, but made from ewes' milk.

Middleham

Middleham square

Route instructions

Plan your walk

Barnard Castle
Brough
Kirkby Lonsdale
Skipton
Clitheroe
Ilkley
Keighley
Bradford
Blackburn
Burnley

DISTANCE: 2½ miles (4 km)

TIME: 1¼ hours

START/END: SE127877
To join the walk, park near the market square in Middleham

TERRAIN: Easy

MAPS:
OS Explorer 302;
OS Landranger 99

A From the market square, follow the lane on the left of the castle southwards into open fields. Keep the boundary wall on your right beyond the house at the lane end.

1 The imposing ruins of the Norman castle are worth viewing from within and also from the lane end. Richard III (1452-1485), having reigned for only two years, lost not only his horse and the Battle of Bosworth, but also the Crown of England in 1485, and his successor, Henry Tudor, had no wish to own Middleham. Along with the unhappy memories of his rival, it was abandoned and languished for 161 years. However, because it retained its obvious

potential as a fortress, Cromwell's troops made it untenable in 1646, during the Civil War. Its ruins later became a free quarry for ready-dressed stones and many of the older houses in the town are probably built from materials taken from the castle. The castle is now in the care of English Heritage.

Another feature in the town is St Alkelda's Well, the martyred Saxon princess who died at the hands of the Danes rather than renounce her Christian beliefs. It is her name to which the parish church is dedicated. In the market place and near the Swine Cross, there is a ring where bulls were once tied for the

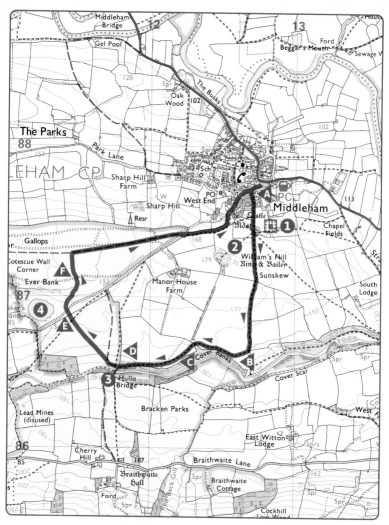

cruel sport of bull-baiting. During his training to become a knight, Richard met and married Anne, the daughter of Richard Neville who was better known as Warwick the Kingmaker. Through Anne, he became owner of Middleham and spent many happy hours indulging in the royal sport of hunting game throughout the Dales. Edward, Richard's only legitimate son, was born in Middleham but died aged 12. His room can be seen in the castle ruins. King Richard, since his portrayal

Middleham

by Shakespeare in Richard III, has been looked upon as an evil king but recent research sees him otherwise. It is in this light that we can think of him as a lover of the Dales, especially Coverdale and his beloved Middleham Castle.

2 A mound which tops the rising field on the right predates the castle and is the earth base of an earlier timber fortification which was abandoned when the main castle was built.

B Bear right towards the trees lining deep-cut Coverdale. Follow the woodland boundary fence as far as a clump of pine trees.

C Climb two stiles at the edge of the wood. Bear half-left, downhill across the next field.

D Walk down to an old, but well-built bridge. Do not cross the river but turn right, away from the bridge and climb along a well-defined cart track.

3 Hullo Bridge. Its stone arch dates back to the times when it was used by heavier traffic than cattle or the occasional tractor and probably carried a coach road south across Coverdale to the interesting 17th century farmhouse of Braithewaite Hall. Parts of the two riverside fields south of Hullo Bridge are available for picnicking or strolling under the 'Countryside Stewardship' scheme.

E Follow the track up to the unfenced Coverdale road. Cross the road and follow red posts up to walk on the pathless grassy swathe of Middleham Moor.

4 The attractive pond on the left is a popular picnic spot. Horses can often be seen being exercised on the nearby common.

F Cross the moor, then bear right, back towards the road. Turn left and follow the road into Middleham.

Middleham from the Tower

> **❝** This quiet walk, often used by locals, is a pleasant alternative to the better-known areas of the Dales **❞**

This walk is in a quiet section of rural Coverdale. The paths are mainly those used by locals for their evening or Sunday afternoon strolls and provide a pleasant alternative to the better-known areas of the Yorkshire Dales. The walk starts and finishes in Carlton. You can park near the Forester's Arms in this small farming village on the minor road linking Middleham and Kettlewell. To the south, not far from Kettlewell, is Park Rash one of the steepest hill climbs in England with a 25% gradient (1 in 4).

Coverdale

Coverdale

Plan your walk

Barnard Castle
Brough
Kirkby Lonsdale
Skipton
Ilkley
Clitheroe Keighley
Bradford
Blackburn Burnley

DISTANCE: 4½ miles (7.2 km)

TIME: 2¼ hours

START/END: SE068847 Carlton

TERRAIN: Easy

MAPS:
OS Explorer OL 30;
OS Landranger 99

Route instructions

A From your parking place near the Forester's Arms, walk east away from the village centre. Turn right along narrow Quaker Lane, signposted to the Rover Cover and West Scrafton.

B Follow the direction of a fingerpost to the right across meadowland.

1 Viewpoint of deep-cut Goodman's Gill and the main valley of Coverdale.

C Follow Goodman's Gill downstream and cross the River Cover by its twin footbridges.

D Climb up the next field as far as a wooded side stream and then bear right on to a faint path across a series of fields leading to West Scrafton. Turn right through the village.

2 Viewpoint. The long line of Carlton's sturdy cottages and farm houses line the opposite hillside.

3 Holes in the garden wall of the end cottage in West Scrafton once held straw beehives. The name Scrafton means the 'town by the hollow' in Saxon and presumably Coverdale is the hollow. The village is a tight packed group of houses around a tiny village green, an ideal base for exploring the lesser-known fells surrounding Scrafton Moor and Great Haw.

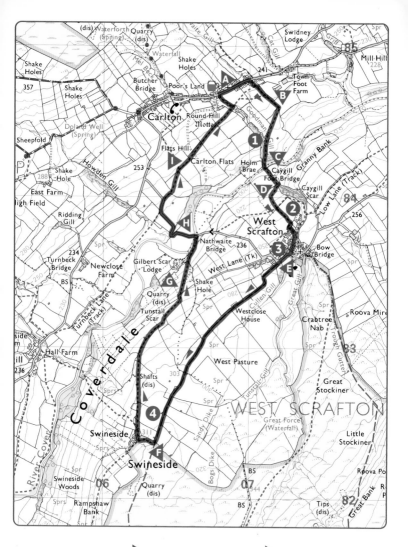

E Turn left and walk along the road to Swineside.

4 Viewpoint of Upper Coverdale, with Little Whernside on your left and Buckden Pike to the right.

F Turn right and follow the lane into Swineside. Go through a gate behind the hotel and bear right, diagonally downhill through a series of fields. Use stiles and gates to follow the correct route.

Coverdale

G Keep to the right above Gilbert Scar Lodge and then walk down its access drive to the road. Turn left and cross the bridge.

H Walk uphill along the road. At a signpost to Carlton, turn right through a stone stile and climb through several fields using stiles in their boundary walls.

I Follow the field path to a farm track. Cross it, then cross a stream. Turn left on a path back to the main road.

Coverdale

Coverdale

> 66 Lovely riverside walk up Wharfedale between Kettlewell and Starbotton; particularly pretty in spring and summer 99

Here is an easy, low-level walk connecting two attractive Upper Wharfedale villages. From Kettlewell on the B6160, a field path, which is centuries old, links it with Starbotton. The return is by a riverside path downstream along the Wharfe. There is a car park near the river in Kettlewell.

Kettlewell & Starbotton

Kettlewell

Barnard Castle
Brough
Kirkby Lonsdale
Skipton
Clitheroe
Ilkley
Keighley
Bradford
Blackburn
Burnley

Route instructions

A From the car park, walk towards Kettlewell church. Turn left at the King's Head for about 20yds (18m), passing the youth hostel. Turn right along a grassy lane.

1 Viewpoint. Kettlewell fits snugly above the junction of Cam Gill Beck and the River Wharfe. The name Kettlewell is Old Norse and means either 'Bubbling Spring' or 'Kettil's Well'.

B Climb the stile at the lane head and turn left to follow the boundary wall.

2 The smaller 'in-by' fields on the left are enclosed for use either as hay meadows or for breeding spring lambs.

Larger fields on the right lead out towards the open upland grazing areas.

C Cross all intervening boundary walls by their stiles.

D Go left through a metal gate. Then turn half-right, to walk downhill towards Starbotton village.

3 Starbotton. The Fox & Hounds, a little way along the main road, makes a convenient half-way resting place on this walk. Starbotton is a corruption of Stannerbotton, Old Norse meaning 'the valley where the stakes were cut'.

E Cross the road and follow the walled lane down to the river.

DISTANCE: 4½ miles (7.2 km)

TIME: 2¼ hours

START/END: SD969722 Kettlewell

TERRAIN: Easy

MAPS:
OS Explorer OL 2;
OS Landranger 98

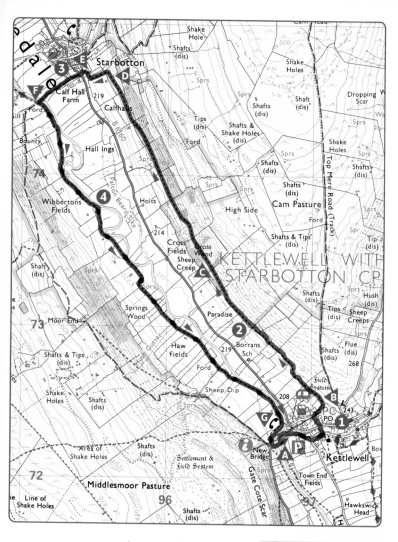

F Cross the footbridge and turn left, downstream through a series of meadows. The path above the river meanders so always use stiles to keep to the correct route.

4 The riverside path is part of the Dales Way long-distance path between Ilkley and Bowness on Lake Windermere. The route is along Wharfedale, then by way of the moors of Cam End and Gearstones into

Kettlewell & Starbotton

verdant Dentdale. Beyond Dentdale, the path skirts the southern foot of the Howgill Fells and leaves North Yorkshire by crossing the Crook of Lune close to the M6. The Cumbrian section of the Dales Way is through Burneside near Kendal and then over a range of low fells to the west of Staveley to reach Windermere at the end of what is considered the most scenic of all the long distance footpaths.

▶ Follow the curve of the riverbank below Kettlewell. Turn left over the double road bridge to reach the village.

Stone bridge at Kettlewell

> **"Passing through Grass Wood you may see a variety of flora and fauna including lily of the valley, wood anemone and wild garlic; and if you walk quietly you may spot some of the local roe deer"**

This walk is from Grassington, 'capital' of the Dales and location of one the Yorkshire Dales National Park Centres. Grassington is a small town with a mixture of architectural styles, including many fine Georgian dwellings and, although it grew with the fortunes of nearby lead mines, its foundations are much older. The town suffered during the period of Scottish border raids in the 14th and later centuries but worse by far was the visitation of the Black Death plague in 1349, when over a quarter of the population in the vicinity of Grassington died. The Grassington Folk Museum of farming and local industry is in the cobbled town square. There are two car parks in Grassington. The largest is near the Information Centre off the B6265 Pateley Bridge road.

River Wharfe
'The Strid'

Ghaistrill's Strid & Grass Wood

Towards Grassington

Route instructions

A From the centre of Grassington. walk along the Conistone road towards the outskirts of the town. Turn left down Wharfe Lane and follow the signposted path as far as Grassington Bridge.

B Turn right and follow the River Wharfe upstream.

1 Ghaistrill's Strid. An attractive picnic site next to a narrow river channel of strangely carved limestone rocks. Do not attempt to jump the Strid (Stride) as the Wharfe flows deep and fast.

C Climb away from the river through an area of natural woodland. Then turn left along the road for ¼ mile (400m).

D Climb the stile next to a gate on the right and enter Grass Wood.

2 Grass Wood Nature Reserve is owned and maintained by the Yorkshire Wildlife Trust. Visitors are allowed to use the right of way through the wood but are expected to observe a few simple rules and respect the wildlife of this unique woodland habitat. Many varieties of spring flowers, including lily of the valley, wild garlic, wood anemone, solomon's seal and bluebells, as well as much rarer plants, such as early purple orchids, bloom in Grass Wood. Please do not pick any of them as it often kills the parent plant.

Plan your walk

DISTANCE: 4½ miles (7.2 km)

TIME: 2¼ hours

START/END: SE002639 Grassington

TERRAIN: Easy / Moderate: one climb at start of Grass Wood

MAPS: OS Explorer OL 2; OS Landranger 98

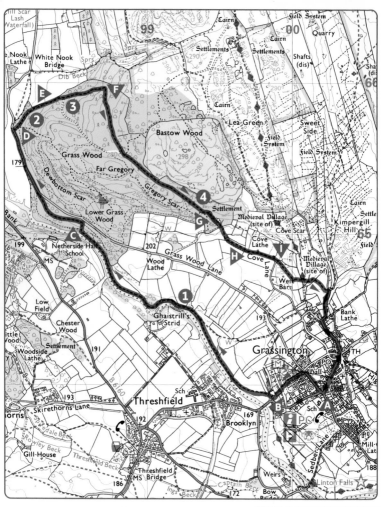

E Continue ahead following the path uphill, ignoring the wider track on the right. The path you are following eventually bears right into denser wood. Follow it for 320yds (290m) beyond the junction.

3 Viewpoint. Dramatic Kilnsey Crag can be seen about 1¼ miles (2km) upstream of this point to the north-west. The crag is a popular climbing area for rock gymnasts but the less energetic can enjoy the Kilnsey Trout Farm and nearby angling pools.

Ghaistrill's Strid & Grass Wood

F Swing right, then bear left onto a woodland track and follow it over the brow of a hill.

4 Viewpoint. Trees have overgrown the ancient settlement but many of its substantial walls can still be traced. Here is an old village which predates Georgian Grassington and was built across what was once an open treeless hillside. The Black Death wiped out most of its inhabitants and the farms and houses were abandoned to nature. Beautiful Grass Wood now covers a scene of sickness and tragedy.

G Keep to the left of the plaque marking the ancient settlement. Go downhill and leave the wood at a ladder stile leading into open meadowland.

H Cross one field and then follow a walled lane running between lush meadows.

I Where the lane makes a sharp bend to the right, climb a flight of stone steps to reach a stile. Go through it into the upper fields and follow the path into Grassington.

Grassington

> The River Aire now runs underground at this point, but before the last ice age a waterfall higher than Niagara cascaded over the impressive 240ft (70m) high cliff at Malham Cove

Most of the thousands of visitors who come to Malham each year do so by following the delightful scenic road which leaves the A65 at Gargrave. The village can get crowded but its fame is justified and the National Park Authority, by careful planning control, has enabled it to retain much of its charm. This walk avoids the more popular routes and uses lesser-known paths to reach the spectacular rock formations of Malham Cove and neighbouring Gordale Scar.

Malham Cove & Gordale Scar

Gordale Scar

Route instructions

1 Malham. A typical Dales' village, it has shops, two pubs and several cafés. The bridge was originally built for pack horses but has been widened to cope with modern traffic.

A From the National Park car park, follow the road to the left through the village, then right over a hump-backed bridge.

B Turn left along the lane in front of the youth hostel. Follow the waymarked path through the fields.

C Go left down to the stream and over a stone clapper bridge. Turn right towards the foot of Malham Cove, then left up the stepped path.

D Follow the limestone pavement to the right, keeping well back from the edge, especially in wet or windy weather. Climb a ladder stile and bear right uphill on a waymarked grassy path.

2 Malham Cove. The stream issuing from the foot of the overhanging limestone crag inspired Charles Kingsley to write his 'Water Babies' novel. Despite appearances to the contrary, this is not the infant River Aire but a stream which has travelled beneath the moors well to the north-west of Malham. The Aire begins its life as Malham Tarn and then disappears underground at Water Sinks, south of the

Plan your walk

DISTANCE: 4¾ miles (7.6 km)

TIME: 2½ hours

START/END: SD900627 Malham

TERRAIN: Moderate / Strenuous; one climb of 377 feet (115m)

MAPS:
OS Explorer OL 2;
OS Landranger 98

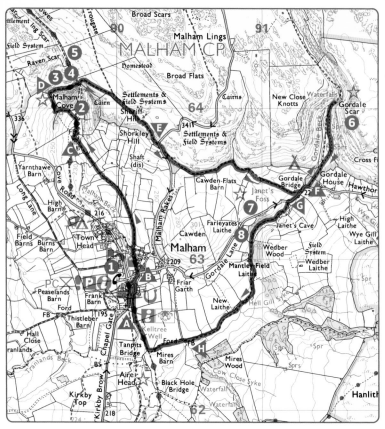

tarn, before resurfacing at Aire Head Springs beyond the village. The main river is, therefore, beneath the stream which appears at the foot of the Cove. Malham Tarn is a unique feature in the normally dry limestone landscape. It owes its occurrence to a layer of impervious rock below the natural depression now filled by the lake. The river has not always been underground. Before the last ice age a waterfall higher than Niagara cascaded over

the 240ft (70m) high cliff of Malham Cove.

3 The bare limestone pavement is fissured by deep north/south aligned 'grikes'. Plants growing in their shady recesses, such as hart's tongue fern and dog's mercury, are associated with the ground cover of an ash wood, which covered most of the fells before the last Ice Age.

4 Viewpoint. Upper Airedale stretches towards

Malham Cove & Gordale Scar

the hazy line of western hills which mark its widest limits. Beyond Gargrave is the Aire-Calder gap. This is a natural break in the Pennines and it has provided a low-level, all-weather route for travellers since prehistoric times. The fields directly below Malham Cove still show the outlines of their medieval pattern.

5 The dry valley on the left is the ancient course of the River Aire before its disappearance underground. A well-made drystone wall follows the dale and marks the boundary between lands belonging to Fountains and Bolton Abbeys. Much of the wealth of these abbeys grew, in medieval times, from lead mining and the extensive sheep walks (grazings).

E Cross ladder stiles on both sides of the road and follow the grassy path downhill.

F Turn left at Gordale Bridge. Follow the signposted streamside path as far as the waterfall and return to this point.

6 There is a cathedral-like atmosphere beneath the towering cliffs of Gordale Scar. The gorge is a collapsed cave system carved by melt water at the end of the last Ice Age. A waterfall now cascades down a cliff composed of tufa, reformed deposits of limestone on moss. The stream flows out of a 'window' in rocks above the fall. It is possible to reach the top of the waterfall and continue the walk out onto Malham Lings moor but it involves a wet and often slippery rock climb up the face of the tufa outcrop. It is safer, therefore, to follow the route as described and return from this point.

G Follow the road for a few yards below Gordale Bridge and go through the gate on the left, which is signposted to Janet's Foss. Follow the woodland stream down towards the open fields.

7 Janet's Foss. The waterfall is created by moss 'fossilised' by tufa deposits which have built up into an attractive green outcrop. Janet is a friendly fairy who lives in the hollow beside the foss. 'Foss' is a Dales word for waterfall and comes from the Old Norse.

8 Wild garlic, bluebells, wood anemones, dog's mercury and violets grow in the shade of the ash woodland.

H Follow signposts along a gravelled path back to Malham.

> **The view of Wharfedale from the rocky outcrop of Simon's Seat make the walk worthwhile**

The best approach is by way of Appletreewick, which is off the B6160. Drive down the Barden Bridge road for ½ mile (0.8km). Park beyond the bridge below Howgill chapel. Appletreewick – the locals pronounce it 'Ap'trick' – has two pubs and both serve food. Several old houses, at least 400 years old, give an indication of the age of this village. It was once classed as a township, being granted a charter in 1311 to hold an annual Onion Fair. Simon's Seat, the high point of this walk, is on Barden Fell grouse moor. Although access is free for most of the year, there will be days when the moor is closed for shooting, or during drought and periods of high fire risk. Check locally with the Bolton Abbey Estate Office (01756 718009) or the Grassington Yorkshire Dales National Park Centre (01756 751690).

Descent to Wharfedale
from Simon's Seat

Simon's Seat

Appletreewick

Route instructions

A From the bridge, turn left along the sandy lane into Howgill.

B Go left along the farm lane, passing the camp site.

1 Viewpoint. Barden's woodlands cloak Lower Wharfedale with Barden Moor as their backcloth. Fir Beck joins the main dale directly below the viewpoint. Parcevall Hall, with its attractive gardens (open to the public during the summer), is upstream of Fir Beck and beyond the hall is Trollers Gill, a narrow ravine with an eerie echo.

C About 100yds (90m) short of Dalehead Farm, go through a gate on the right and climb the path which

winds its way up the bracken-covered hillside.

D Cross a level track and, still climbing, bear right past an oak tree. Look for occasional yellow arrows painted on rocks.

E Scramble leftwards to the rocky summit of Simon's Seat.

2 Viewpoint. The view makes the climb worthwhile. Wharfedale cuts a deep winding trough to the north and the broad spread of Ilkley Moor is to the south.

F Turn right, away from the rocks, and follow the steadily descending path across the moor as

Plan your walk

DISTANCE: 4 miles (6.4km)

TIME: 2 hours

START/END: SE059592 Layby parking just before Howgill Chapel, very close to the village of Appletreewick.

TERRAIN: Strenuous; one climb of 1122 feet (342m)

MAPS:
OS Explorer 298;
OS Landranger 98, 99 & 104

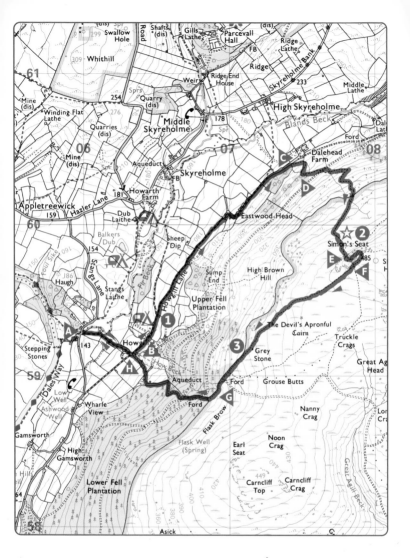

indicated by a signpost to Howgill and Barden.

3 Viewpoint of the hamlet and farmsteads of Howgill sheltering below a tree-covered hillock.

G Bear right, downhill, on a rocky path and through a plantation of pine trees.

H Cross Howgill Lane and rejoin the track down to the road bridge.

Simon's Seat

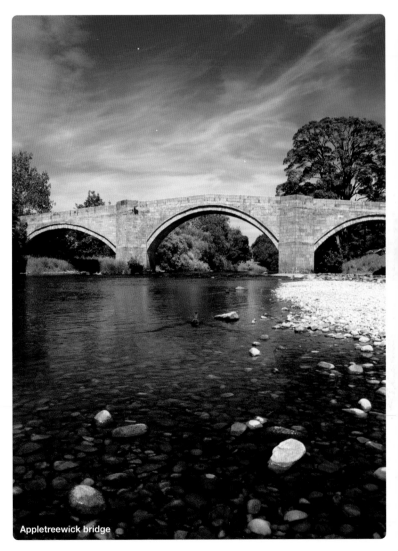

Appletreewick bridge

> **❝** In the caves of Attermire Scar traces of human habitation from prehistoric times have been found **❞**

The walk starts from the centre of Settle, 'capital' of Upper Ribblesdale. This is a busy market town on the A65 with parking near the market place. Settle is also the southern terminus of the scenic Settle to Carlisle railway. Although the line is historic and runs chartered steam trains on special occasions, it is part of the National Rail Network with regular timetables. Soon after leaving the bustle of the town, steep but easy-to-follow paths climb to the limestone wilderness of Attermire Scar. Several small caves penetrate its craggy lower slopes. A torch is desirable if you plan to explore their depths. The return is by a gently descending field track with wide-ranging views of Ribblesdale and the Craven district.

Attermire Scar

Attermire Scar

Plan your walk

DISTANCE: 5 miles (8km)

TIME: 2½ hours

START/END: SD819636 Settle

TERRAIN: Moderate / Strenuous; total climb of 700 feet (213m)

MAPS: OS Explorer OL 2; OS Landranger 98

Route instructions

A Follow the road to the left of the market place and climb towards Constitution Hill.

B Bear right, away from the road and follow the rough-walled lane uphill.

C About 100yds (90m) beyond a clump of trees, turn right at a signpost to Malham. Climb the grassy hillside. At first, there is no path but one soon develops. Follow this to the right of the boundary wall.

1 Viewpoint across the townscape of Settle and the Ribble Valley with the Ingleborough fells on the right.

2 Viewpoint. The limestone crags of Attermire Scar, the surface indication of the line of a major geological fault, fill the steep hillside on your left giving it the appearance of a much higher mountain. Malham Moor is directly ahead.

D Cross a stile and then go through a gap in the wall. Turn left and climb the rocky path along the foot of the crags.

3 The caves of Attermire Scar. Attermire Cave is just north of point **D** and four small caves surround Victoria Cave near the highest point of the climb. Jubilee Cave, so named because of its discovery

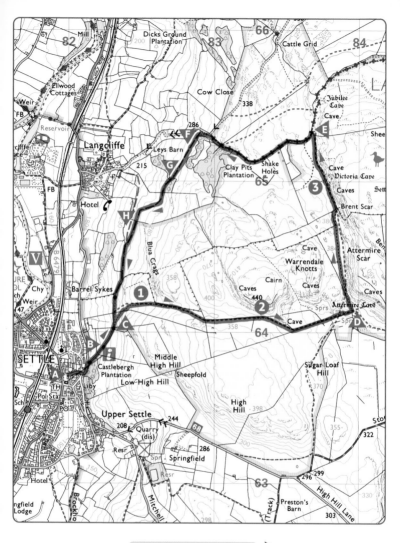

at the time of Queen Victoria's Jubilee, is about 110yds (101m) uphill beyond point **E**. Traces of habitation from prehistoric to post-Roman times have been found in some of the caves.

E Turn left through a metal gate and follow the well-made farm track downhill.

F At the point where the track joins the road, turn left through a small gate and follow a field path along the

Attermire Scar

bottom edge of a mature wood.

 Use the gate in the narrow gap between two sections of woodland.

 Take the stile at the side of the wicket gate. Walk ahead along a field path and descend by an improving track into the outskirts of Settle.

The Ribble valley from Langcliffe Scar

> *A geological treat: this walk up Pen-y-ghent, with its clear horizontal rock strata, takes you through geological time from the carboniferous limestones at the base, through sandstones and shales to the millstone grit summit*

Pen-y-ghent is one of the few real peaks in the Pennines. Most of the other summits are simply the highest points in an area of wild moorland. Here we have one of the most graceful English mountains. Its slopes benignly dominate Horton in Ribblesdale, a busy village on the B6479 and the starting place for this ascent of Pen-y-ghent. Horton is also the usual start and finishing point for the gruelling race, or individual attempts, on the 'Three Peaks', of which Pen-y-ghent is one. The other two are Whernside, above the graceful span of Ribblehead Viaduct north-west of Horton, and Ingleborough, to the south of Whernside and closer to Horton. The distance involved is about 24 miles (38.6km) and has been completed in under four hours by fell runners but ordinary walkers need over 12 hours of daylight for safety.

Double ladder stile
on Pen-y-ghent

Pen-y-ghent

Pen-y-ghent

Route instructions

A The walk starts at the car park on the B6479 diagonally opposite the Crown Hotel. Walk south, past the church and then left on a side road following Douk Ghyll stream.

1 Horton church. A typical Dales church. Its roof is made from locally mined lead and the flags of its floor are made of slate taken from nearby quarries. The doorway is Norman but the beautiful stained glass window in its south wall is modern. Pillars dividing the nave slope to the south – a curious traditional feature of the area.

B Turn left at Brackenbottom Farm and follow the signposted footpath uphill. Cross all walls by their stiles.

2 A wooden walkway is helping prevent further erosion on boggy stretches of the climb.

C Climb over the stile and turn left to join the Pennine Way path, which you follow steeply uphill. Scramble though the craggy gritstone outcrops and follow the wide path towards the summit cairn.

3 Viewpoint. Whernside and Ingleborough are across the Ribble Valley. Fountains Fell, to the south-east, is crossed by the Pennine Way, which has climbed Pen-y-ghent from Dale Head to the

Plan your walk

DISTANCE: 6 miles (9.7km)

TIME: 3 hours

START/END: SD807725 Horton in Ribblesdale

TERRAIN: Strenuous; muddy sections; one climb of 1522ft (464m)

MAPS: OS Explorer OL 2; OS Landranger 98

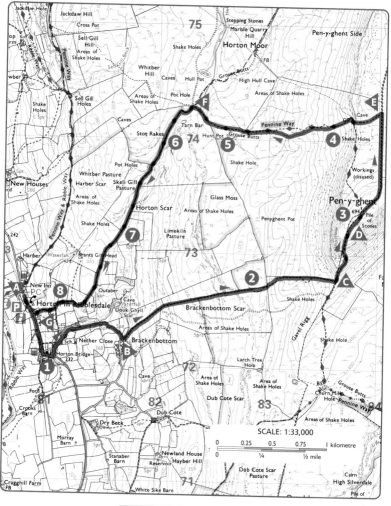

south of Fawcett Moor, before descending to Horton. The various strata or bands of rock which make Pen-y-ghent's distinctive shape are clearly defined on the climb from Brackenbottom. Limestone gives way, in turn, to sandstone, shales and eventually, millstone grit on the summit. All the rocks were laid down in a tropical sea which became inundated by a muddy river delta. Vertical crags and detached pinnacles feature on the steepest part of the mountain while, lower down, the relatively flat moor is

Pen-y-ghent

dotted with pot holes and sinks where streams disappear. They reappear in the valley bottom closer to the village, which sits on a layer of impervious silurian slate.

 Climb the ladder stile to reach the summit. Leave by a wide path, which slants to the right, down the rocky slope.

4 Notice the detached limestone pinnacle beyond the footpath junction. Alpine purple saxifrage hangs from the limestone crags in April and early May.

 Turn sharp left at the path junction and go steeply down towards the boggy moor.

5 Hunt Pot. This deep pothole is a few yards to the left of the path. Take great care as the rock around its lip is very slippery. Water flowing into the dark depths of Hunt Pot reappears as Brants Gill, near the Crown Hotel. Douk Ghyll, the stream which you followed from Horton Church, flows from Hull Pot to the north-

west of Hunt Pot, the two streams managing to cross each other underground.

 Turn left through a gate at the side of a ruined shooting cabin. Follow the walled lane downhill.

6 The lane is one of the ancient green roads of the Pennines. This one was a packhorse way, linking Ribblesdale and Littondale.

7 Ever-changing views of Pen-y-ghent standing proudly above its dramatic limestone moors, can be enjoyed almost all the way down to Horton in Ribblesdale.

8 Viewpoint. Ingleborough is opposite, marred only by the ugly intrusion of Horton Quarry, reminding us of the price we must pay for good road surfaces.

 The lane joins the B6479 conveniently close to the Pen-y-ghent Café. Turn right down the road to return to the car park on the left.

Pen-y-ghent

66 With its stark moorland landscape situated
away from the usual tourist trail this quiet
area of the Dales offers great solitude **99**

Wild Upper Littondale is one of the least visited places in the
Dales. A tributary of Wharfedale, its stark moorland solitude
contrasts with more popular areas. The valley road leaves the
B6160 at Skirfare Bridge between Kettlewell and Kilnsey and
makes a sharp turn at Halton Gill to climb beneath Pen-y-ghent
on its way to Staniforth. A short cul-de-sac road from Halton Gill
continues for about a mile to Foxup and it is from here that the
walk starts. Roadside parking is limited but a few spaces can
usually be found near Foxup Bridge.

Upper Littondale

River Skirfare

Route instructions

1 Notice how the sturdy farmhouses at Foxup have been built with their backs to the cold north wind.

A Turn left opposite Foxup Bridge Farm and go through a gate. Climb the grassy track signposted to Horton in Ribblesdale.

B Bear left, away from the wall as indicated by a signpost. Follow the path away from the wall to a gate.

C Turn right along the metalled road and follow it for about 600yds (550m).

2 Viewpoint. Looking down Littondale towards Wharfedale in the hazy distance.

3 Viewpoint. Pen-y-ghent can be seen ahead with Fountains Fell on the left.

D Turn sharp left at a signpost and follow a wire fence diagonally downhill to Nether Heselden Farm.

4 Viewpoint. The deep ravine of Pen-y-ghent Gill is on the right. The trees along the river bank are remnants of forests which covered the Dales before the last Ice Age.

E Go through the farmyard and turn left. Then go through a gate at the side of a large circular slurry tank. Follow the signposted route across a series of fields.

Plan your walk

Barnard Castle
Brough
Kirkby Lonsdale
Skipton
Ilkley
Clitheroe   Keighley
Bradford
Blackburn   Burnley

DISTANCE: 4 miles (6.4 km)

TIME: 2 hours

START/END: SD872767 Foxup

TERRAIN: Moderate

MAPS:
OS Explorer OL 2;
OS Landranger 98

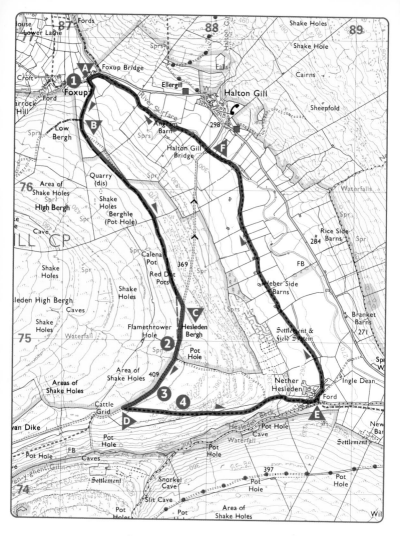

Cross the road to the left of Halton Gill Bridge. Continue by riverside field path to Foxup Bridge.

Upper Littondale

Ladder Stile, Littondale

66 This easy walk circles Feetham and follows the elevated riverbank of the River Swale **99**

The route of the walk is an irregular oval centred on Feetham, which is roughly 3¾ miles (6km) west of Reeth along the B6270 in central Swaledale. As parking near the start of the walk is limited, it will probably be better to leave the car in Feetham. A visit to The Punch Bowl Inn in Feetham is recommended after completing this pleasant walk.

Walls and barns in Swaledale

Central Swaledale

Swaledale

Route instructions

A The walk starts from the B6270 opposite a solitary barn about ½ mile (0.8km) east of Feetham. Climb the steep tree-lined track. It is difficult to follow in its upper reaches but keep to the left of the stream without climbing any walls.

1 Viewpoint. Looking down Swaledale and across the heather-clad Grinton Moors.

B Turn left at the top of the rise and join a farm track.

2 Gallows Top Farm; named after a gibbet which stood nearby.

C Cross the moorland road and follow the direction of a signpost across rough pastureland to Blades.

Look out for stiles to keep on course.

3 Viewpoint. Looking east towards a wooded section of the central dale.

D Bear left, then right for about 40yds (37m) along the road. Go left through the second gate beyond the roadside house. Follow a line of stiles diagonally right, down a series of fields.

4 Blades. A typical Yorkshire Dales' hill settlement. Look for the date over the door of the last house on the right of the path.

5 Each spring, purple orchids grow near the stream below Turnip House.

Plan your walk

DISTANCE: 3¾ miles (6km)

TIME: 2 hours

START/END: SD994985 Opposite a solitary barn on the B6270 half a mile east of Feetham.

TERRAIN: Easy; one climb of 354 feet (108m)

MAPS: OS Explorer OL 30; OS Landranger 91, 92 & 98

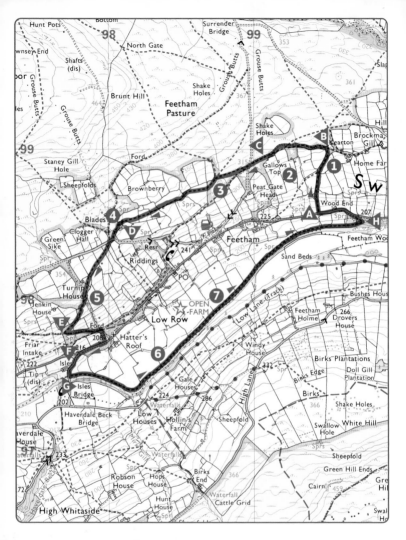

E Turn left on a rough track and follow it downhill. Cross a ford and just after, turn right and descend on a path through a wood. Turn right along the road.

F Bear left at the road

junction and go down to the bridge.

G Cross the stile beside the ruined gate on the nearside of the bridge and turn left downstream, along the elevated riverbank.

Central Swaledale

6 The Swale drains a large area of moor to the north and west and can quickly reach alarming proportions, hence the need for such a high embankment.

7 Viewpoint. Feetham stands on its sunny terrace well above the danger of flooding.

H At the signpost, go left away from the river and climb through trees to reach the road. Turn left back towards Feetham.

Swaledale

> **"Spring is the best time to appreciate this walk when the water levels are high and the delicate green of the newly leafed trees form a lovely backdrop through which you can glimpse views of the deeper ravines"**

This is probably the most beautiful walk in the Yorkshire Dales. For most of the way, the footpath, first opened to the public in 1885, is privately owned and, as a result, an admission fee is charged. Most of the ground covered is in an Area of Special Scientific Interest being of geological and botanical interest.

Two rivers, the Doe and Twiss, join below Ingleton to become the Greta, itself a tributary of the Lune, one of the two Dales' rivers flowing into the Irish Sea (the other is the Ribble). Upstream from Ingleton, the Doe and Twiss, after originating on the opposite side of Whernside, flow through flat-bottomed upper valleys before cascading down treelined limestone gorges. The walk follows their course in a clockwise direction, upstream along the Twiss, then down the Doe.

Pecca Falls

Ingleton's Waterfalls

Thornton Force

Plan your walk

DISTANCE: 4½ miles (7.2km)

TIME: 2¼ hours

START/END: SD694730 Ingleton. Approach the car park by driving through Ingleton from either the A65 Settle road or the B6255 Hawes road and then follow the side road steeply down into the valley.

TERRAIN: Moderate; slippery areas when wet; one climb of 500 feet (152m)

MAPS:
OS Explorer OL 2;
OS Landranger 98

Route instructions

A▷ Follow the wide footpath away from the car park, upstream through tree-lined Swilla Glen.

1 The outward section of the walk follows the River Twiss upstream. Its waterfalls tend to be wider than the Doe's and are best seen face on. Those of the Doe are mostly in tree-lined narrow ravines, which are more dramatic when viewed from above. Both rivers join a few yards below the road which leads into the car park.

2 Pecca Falls, a series of narrow cascades. Refreshments are on sale during the summer from a hut on the hillside.

3 Thornton Force. The highest waterfall – 46ft (14m) – in the Ingleton area and, many would say, the most attractive. The tree fringed limestone crag makes a natural amphitheatre. The darker rock beneath the falls is slate which, unlike limestone, is impervious to water.

B▷ Cross the footbridge and climb towards the open field.

C▷ Turn right along a narrow farm lane to Twistleton Hall.

D▷ Follow the signposted footpath away from the farm, down to and over the Chapel-le-Dale road.

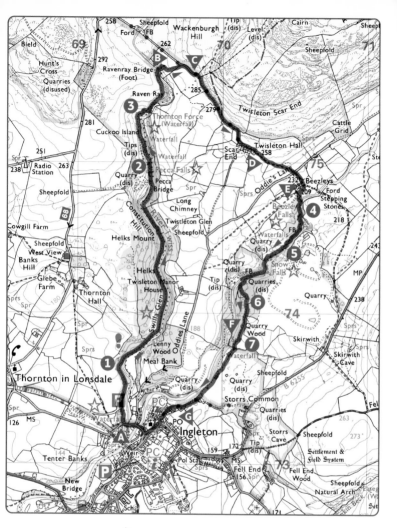

Go past Beezleys Farm and then follow a signposted footpath to the right, into the narrowing valley.

4 Beezley Falls. The first cascade of the hitherto peaceful River Doe. Outcrops and boulders in the river-bed cause the stream to make several dramatic changes of its direction.

5 Snow Falls. One of a series of three falls in the section of the valley known as Twistleton Glen.

Ingleton's Waterfalls

6 The quarry, here, once exploited the harder but more easily worked slate which forms the bed-rock of this normally limestone region.

▶ Join an improving track away from the old quarry.

7 Cat Leap Fall. A little off route, on the left, this fall is the final exuberant act of Skirwith Beck, a side stream which joins the Doe close by an old limestone quarry.

G Bear left into the centre of Ingleton, past the church and then turn right, down the road to the car park.

Beezley Falls

> **❝** Ideal all-weather walk which follows a route using farm lanes **❞**

The walk starts near the chapel which gives the hamlet of Chapel-le-Dale its name. Access is by the side road which leaves the B6255 below the Hill Inn and is about 3½ miles (5.6km) north-east of Ingleton. As the route is entirely along farm lanes, it is suitable in all weathers.

The path to Ingleborough from Chapel-le-Dale

Chapel-le-Dale

Ribblehead Viaduct

Plan your walk

Barnard Castle
Brough
Kirkby Lonsdale
Skipton
Ilkley
Clitheroe Keighley
Bradford
Blackburn Burnley

DISTANCE: 3½ miles (5.6km)

TIME: 1¾ hours

START/END: SD737771 Chapel-le-Dale. Car parking is available opposite the church.

TERRAIN: Easy

MAPS:
OS Explorer OL 2;
OS Landranger 98

Route instructions

A Park near St. Leonard's church in Chapel-le-Dale. Turn right behind the church and follow the wooded lane uphill.

1 St. Leonard's church. Inside this simple Dales church is a memorial to the men who died, either from injury or cholera while building Ribblehead Viaduct and the Settle to Dent section of the Leeds to Carlisle railway.

2 Viewpoint. The massive bulk of Ingelborough towers above tree-shrouded Hurtle Pot, which is reputed to be the home of a boggard. A boggard is a Dales' sprite, who can be friendly or mischievous depending on how he is treated.

3 Sculpture piece. A plaque on the unexpected piece of sculpture at the side of the lane tells its story.

4 Viewpoint. Gill Head House makes a pleasant foreground to this view of Ingleborough. Turn around and the long whale-back ridge of Whernside fills the skyline. Ingleborough is composed mostly of limestone but Whernside's rocks are mainly shales and gritstones above a base of limestone which fills the dale on all sides of Chapel-le-Dale.

5 Viewpoint. Ribblehead Viaduct to the north-east. This dramatic man-made feature spanning the dale

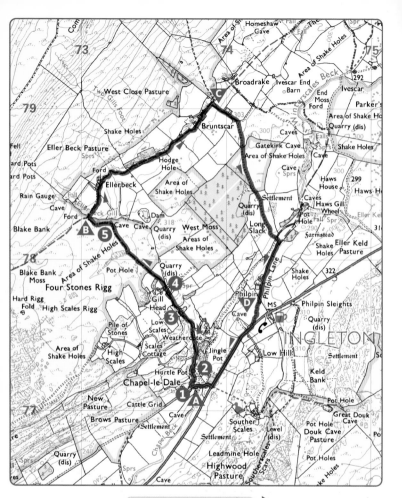

head fits well within the moorland landscape.

B Cross the shallow ford and follow the farm lane to the right. Go through the farmyard and out along a cart track to the right.

C Turn right at a signpost marked 'Hill Inn 1 mile'. Go down the metalled lane.

D At the main road, refreshment is available about 180yds (165m) to the left at the Hill Inn. Otherwise, follow the road to the right, to the side road turning into Chapel-le-Dale.

Chapel-le-Dale

The edge of Twisleton Scar

Photo credits